CLOUD COM[

A to Z of Cloud Computing

Nobert Young

TABLE OF CONTENT

Introduction 4

Chap 1: What is Cloud computing 10

Models of Cloud Computing 13

Chap 2: Cloud Computing Deployment Models and Types 25

Types of Cloud Computing Services 38

Chap 3: Virtualization of Service models 56

Comparing Traditional Servers to Virtual Servers 60

Types of Virtualization 62

Benefits of cloud computing 82

Disadvantages of cloud computing 86

Understanding Cloud Architecture 94

Chap 4: Exploring the Cloud Computing Stack ... 97

Chap 5: Connecting to the Cloud, Cloud Storage and Migration 118

Cloud Storage 121

Migrating to the Cloud 131

Chapter 6: Cloud Computing Security, Business Continuity and Data Recovery 140

Cloud Vulnerability and Penetration Testing 150

Encryption 151

Compliance and Cloud Computing......................154
Business Continuity and Data Recovery 155
Log and Audit Trail...156
In Legal and contractual issues 156
Chap 7: Conclusion..158
Other Books by Same Author.............................159

Introduction

There's a lot of buzz in global tech communities concerning Cloud computing right now. Regardless, there are still lots of people as well as new tech enthusiasts who do not fully grasp what cloud computing is all about.

If you are not clear on what cloud computing is, you probably make up the 95% of people who use cloud services like the social networks and online banking without knowing it.

As we shall see further down, Cloud computing is basically hosting on servers that are not physically present.

Cloud computing is using software and hardware to deliver a service over the internet. With cloud computing, users are able to access files and applications from any available device connected to the internet.

Formerly, website owners put their websites on physical servers to enable their users to gain access to data and /or communicate with other users. Overtime, these dedicated servers tend to get clogged as more and more users access it thus creating a cluster and leading to a slow/ unresponsive website, consequently giving need to buy more hardware servers for hosting and this takes a great deal of time to setup and money to manage given that these servers have to be paid for whether or not they are being used.

Thankfully, Cloud computing offers an almost instant hosting service which saves a large amount of time and costs less since you only pay for what you use and nothing more. Think of it like cab ride with an automated meter, the cost only applies to the ride and not the purchase of the whole cab.

Now, with your website on a cloud server, when clusters set in and you need extra computing power to green-light the traffic, you can increase your server scale almost instantly by purchasing more space.

Cloud computing generally refers to the limitless use of virtual resources which are shared across networks and are easily accessible through standard internet protocols.

In order to ease our interpretation of the ambiguity of Cloud computing, it has been defined in multiple ways along the course of this book with initial focus on two classes of Cloud computing which are:

The deployment model – which shows the location of the Cloud and its designated purpose with sub examples of Public, Private, Community, and Hybrid clouds.

The Service Model – this is basically a description of the services being offered by the service provider. Service models include but are not limited to software, Platforms and Infrastructures all given as a service (The SPI model). These models build on each other and define the responsibilities that belong to the vendor and that which belongs to the client.

Cloud computing indicates a shift in method of system deployments due to the overtime growth and popularity of the internet and service providing companies. It provides the most wanted service requested for by tech users which is a sort of pay-per-use yet easily increasable on an infinite scale whilst being a computing utility with readily available and universal system. Growth with this sort of system is very fast irrespective of the starting size.

It is important to note that problems do arise with latency, transactions, security and regulatory compliances therefore Cloud computing doesn't benefit all applications.

Chap 1: What is Cloud computing

Cloud computing in the simplest term means to store and access data and programs on the internet rather than on your personal hard drive.

The cloud refers to different types of software and hardware that are used collectively to make different aspects of computing available to final users as an online service.

"Cloud" in this context refers to two basic concepts which are:

Abstraction: Cloud is based widely on a virtual system therefore making applications run on unspecified physical systems with data stored in unknown locations, administrative systems outsourced to others and an omnipresent access by users.

Virtualization: Cloud computing acts as a virtual computing system that collects and shares resources whose costs are charged on a metered based basis, therefore giving room for multi-tenancy and scalable resources.

Clouds come in multiple forms. The services in which they provide may or may not be rendered by Cloud service provider. For clarity purposes, here are three examples of Cloud utilizing companies:

Google: A great amount of data centres have been created in the last decade by this prestigious company worldwide. This has enabled Google to control a great deal of advertising revenue generated worldwide which has in turn made possible the free gifting of software to clients given that the Cloud infrastructure has changed the market for user-facing software.

Amazon Web Services: this company offers users her service by letting users rent virtual computers on infrastructures owned by Amazon. It is known to be one of the most successful Cloud based enterprise.

Azure Platform: By Contrast, The Azure platform which is created by Microsoft is built for the enablement of the running of .NET Framework. This platform allows users to build and host solutions using products from Microsoft and from their data centres. It is an all-inclusive collection of cloud products that give users access to create enterprise-class without the need to build a personal infrastructure.

The above stated companies are truly revolutionary given that they enable applications to be executed with the littlest of costs and to be rapidly scaled whilst being available on-demand worldwide.

Models of Cloud Computing

Cloud computing are most commonly separated into two classes which are the most widely accepted sets of Cloud computing. As we had already stated, these classes are the Deployment models and the Service Models. Outside these two mentioned above, we have more models of Cloud computing which I shall breakdown and show you what they do. These models include:

The NIST Model:

The NIST (which is an abbreviation for National Institute of Standards and Technology) located in the U.S is a major user of Cloud computing networks given that the United States is known as one of the biggest countries in consumption of computer and tech services on a large scale.

Originally, the NIST model didn't have need for resource pooling via virtualization of a Cloud, neither was there support of multi-tenancy by a Cloud in the initial definition of Cloud computing. With Cloud computing moving towards a set of interacting components with the Service Oriented Architecture as a good example of the component. Although the NIST Cloud model doesn't take into consideration a good number of services such as transaction or service brokering, interoperability, provisioning and Integration services which are the base topic for Cloud discussion, it is easily expected that future versions of NIST

Cloud model may add these features as well. The up rise in the roles of brokers, Cloud APIs and service buses at different levels, come the increasing need for these elements to be added.

The Cloud Cube Model:

This model which was designed by Jericho Forum is basically made to aid in the choosing of Cloud formations for collaborative security. Intriguingly, IT managers and Business leaders gain access to Cloud computing thanks to this Cloud model.

The Cloud Cube model takes the different "Cloud formations" in view therefore amounting to Cloud deployment and service models. Majority of Cloud providers acknowledge the importance of Cloud security to its consumers, regardless, it is a given that the Cloud customer is responsible for the accountability of the selection of desired Cloud formation to meet their personal regulatory and data location requirements. The higher in hierarchy of a Cloud service model they choose, the more the dependence on the Cloud provider to provide security and data portability ease.

In order to ensure data protection, you first of all need to systematize your data so as to know what rules are applicable to protect it, that way you ensure that you check for data sensitivity and regulatory/compliance restrictions. Once you have the above covered, you're now ready to decide what data and processes need be moved to the Cloud and which needs to be withheld and what levels you want to operate the Cloud given that Cloud models segregate into layers of business service from each other, e.g. Infrastructure/ Platform/ Software/ Process.

The Cloud cube model has 4 dimensions to which the Cloud formations are being differentiated. These are:

a) **External/Internal dimension:** This explains the physical location of data; it lets one know if data you try to access is inside or outside your organization's boundaries. For instance, the use of private Cloud deployment by a data centre is considered as internal while that which resides on Amazon EC2 would be considered external.

b) **The Proprietary/Open dimension:** This refers to the ownership condition/state of Cloud technology, services and interfaces. Through this, the degree of interoperability as well as the enabling of data transportability between your systems or other Cloud forms is well indicated and you'd be able to move data without constraint.

c) **The Perimeterised/ De-Perimeterised dimension:** This is basically the architectural mindset. Perimeterised refers to operation continuity within the traditional IT perimeter, signalled often by 'Network firewalls. When working in the area that is perimeterised, you can easily extend the perimeter of your organization into the external Cloud computing domain by operating the virtual server in your own IP domain using a VPN whilst using your own directory services to control access.

De- perimeterised on the other hand makes an assumption that the system perimeter is architected in accordance to the principles of the Jericho Forum's Commandments and Collaboration Oriented Architecture Framework. Data is compressed with meta-data in a de-perimeterised frame; thus, the data is protected with the mechanism to prevent it from inappropriate usage. The Cloud cube model areas which are de-perimeterised implement both internal and external domains, but sharing or collaboration of data is rather controlled by parties that organization selects to use (and are limited to these) and not defined as merely internal or external. For example if an organization feels uncomfortable about sharing certain data into the internal COA-compliant domain of a collaborating organization, they will be confident that these data will be appropriately protected using a system of encryption and key management technology to provide data confidentiality and integrity, which would also provide legal safe-harbour when the information is lost or stolen.

d) Insourced/Outsourced dimension: this describes how the delivery of cloud services you consume is being managed. It is basically a "who runs your Cloud?" situation. If the service is provided for by you or your own staff, then the service is insourced meanwhile if the provision comes from a third-party it is said to be outsourced.

There are three key questions every client should ask their cloud suppliers as suggested by the Jericho forum. This would help assure the clients on the security and protection of their data. These are:

- What is the assurance that my data stored in the Cloud services will still be available regardless of whether or not the provider changes in business direction or folds up?

- Which of the cube model is the supplier operating from in providing the cloud computing service?
- Can my supplier assure me that the features I use will be maintained on the long run?

There's a high amount of value placed on the importance of business managers understanding why and how making use of any Cloud form will give added value to their business goals.

Chap 2: Cloud Computing Deployment Models and Types

As earlier stated, a Deployment model is that which defines a Cloud's purpose and the nature of its location.

The deployment models as defined by NIST are:

The Private Cloud:

This model serves mostly companies as this type of cloud computing services is inaccessible by the public. It might exist on or off the organization's physical locations but can only be operated solely the same company. Currently known as the most secure Cloud, the private cloud processes data controlled and managed exclusively for the company without any limitation of network bandwidth, disclosure of security, and any other requirements. In the private cloud, the fundamental Cloud infrastructure could be possibly owned, operated and even managed by the company itself and/or a third-party. It gives room to too many outcomes aiding a public cloud computing environment, for example, becoming a service-based also elastic. Examples Amazon Virtual Private Cloud.

Private clouds are classified into two (2) variations which are:

The On-Premise Private Cloud

This type of private Cloud, also known as the internal Cloud, uniformly offers additional procedure plus security, but frequently runs into restrictions in terms of size and scalability. Plus, an organization's Information Technology (IT) unit would be laboured with the capital and operational costs for the physical resources with this model. Applications which facilitate total control and configurability of the different infrastructures and security are those this type of private cloud is best utilized for.

The Externally-Hosted Private Cloud

The externally-hosted private Cloud is a type of private Cloud model with its Cloud computing provider being held on the outside. This Cloud computing service provider allows for a restriction-based environment with absolute confidentiality guarantee. For organizations that don't make use of public Cloud infrastructure this type of Cloud is easily suggested to them due to the risks affiliated with the physical sharing of resources.

Some characteristics of this private Cloud include:

- **Resource Dedication:** with this type of Cloud, data is easily set aside and dedicated to owning enterprises.
- **Enhancement in security measures:** obviously we know that security is the biggest issue and client concern in the data sharing field. This Cloud model is well designed and equipped with a vast amount of state-of-the-art security and

confidentiality tools poised to guarantee absolute safety.

- **Better customization:** adaptability and customizable user interface is a key factor that makes this cloud computing model preferred by organizations and enterprises. Businesses are able to control and keep track of their data while maintaining data security at same time.

The Public Cloud:

These are owned and managed by companies that offer quick access to cheap computing resources over a public network. Users of public cloud services are not required to purchase software, hardware or any other supporting infrastructure as this is owned by the service providers.

This Cloud model is based on a pay-as-you-go basis, therefore making it one of the easiest to setup as users aren't burdened with the task of setting up equipment. With this model, organizations only have to pay for the services they use alone. It requires no hardware device setup therefore saving the user time and money that can be invested into productivity rather than worry and management of hardware.

This cloud type is famous for its easiness in availability to the general public or a bigger institution. Regardless of its nature, clients' data are not exposed to public view.

Characteristics of this type of Cloud are:

Metered payment: because most businesses are looking for ways to cut cost while maximizing productivity, this model helps companies to achieve this as charges are only on utilized services.

Reliability and availability: ability to remain agile while being easily accessible is a desirable Cloud computing characteristic which is part of what makes this Cloud model-type widely sort after. With this, clients choose their time of convenience (which can be anytime and any day of the week) and are charged for only the times they use the services offered.

Environmental Flexibility and Elasticity: public Cloud services such as Google app engine and Amazon elastic Cloud computing serves its customers immensely by utilizing an adaptable Cloud environment which puts the power of choosing what data to share and how to share in the hands of the clients.

Self-Service: Due to the pre-configuration existing on this cloud, it makes it easy for users to operate and manage without help from the service providers. Clients do not need to be dependent on the service providers or 3rd party to ensure this feature.

The Hybrid Cloud:

This cloud type combines the foundation of the private cloud and the strategic integration and use of the public cloud services. This type of Cloud can be managed internally and privately or by a third party with hosts situated inside or outside. In reality, it is difficult for a private cloud to exist away from the rest of the company's IT resources and public cloud. Hybrid cloud is created when companies with private clouds evolve to manage their workloads across private clouds, data centers and public cloud. This would help to reduce cost of managing private cloud as cost is split amongst all the organizations and users. Regardless of the issues concerning interoperability and Cloud standardization, organizations can still have their security and costs at a reasonable level.

The characteristics of this hybrid Cloud includes:

- **Optimal use/ cutting of cost:** The hybrid cloud is known for helping organizations cut cost. Instead of investing in building of infrastructure to withstand irregular bursts in system usage that rarely happens, organizations can make use of the public cloud to lay off some heavy usage and only pay for when they need it.

- **Consolidation of data centers:** A private cloud requires resources in typical cases as opposed to giving capacity to the most sceptical situation or circumstances. Given to the above stated, the power, maintenance, service costs, cooling as well as hardware are well incorporated.
- **Risk transfer:** the dangers inherent in the error of underestimating workload is transferred to the Cloud seller from the service operator thanks to the proper utilization of the Hybrid Cloud. Although Organizations are personally

maintaining and running their servers and private clouds, the service provider of the public Cloud on the other hand must ensure an extreme uptime for rendered services. Quite clearly, majority of the Cloud providers own the SLAs, to which an uptime of more than 99% is guaranteed consistently.

- **Availability:** accessibility to corporate data centres can be quite cumbersome and costly due to the redundancy and reinforcement of data as well geographical locations. Particularly, these skillsets are usually restricted in organizations where Information Technology is not the primary focus. For hybrid cloud, the public cloud tends to go up in scale size or completely take over operations in situations where the organization's data center unavailable due to some failures and some attacks of Distributed Denial of Service (DDoS).

Community Cloud:

This infrastructure, the community Cloud, is supervised then put into utilization by a good number of institutions that seek and/or have similar core businesses, projects or shareable demand infrastructures which include but are not limited to aspects like software and hardware so that the IT costs can be sufficiently reduced. Therefore, this Cloud becomes manageable by either the joined institutions or the cloud service provider. A very good example of a community Cloud is an academic Cloud.

Types of Cloud Computing Services

There are three well known and widely accepted cloud computing services and these are:

    i.   Software as a Service (SaaS)
    ii.   The Platform as a Services (PaaS)
    iii.   Infrastructure as a Service (IaaS)

These Cloud computing service types are designed with consideration to modern day data centers and has integrated the three service types listed above, provided to them as utilities by enabling consumers to pay for only what they use (pay-as-you-go). The clouds run on Data hardware provided by the Data centers, and these form the foundation of the Cloud. Basically, Data centers are built out of numerous servers linked with each other; and are sited in thickly clustered bands, where the risk of a natural disaster is greatly reduced.

The Software as a Service (SaaS):

Software as a Service (SaaS) is the software distribution model that allows third party providers to host applications as well as make them accessible to customers over the internet. SaaS can be linked to the **On-Demand Computing** and **Application Service Provider (ASP)** software delivery models where the cloud owners host a single software and delivers to multiple end users over the internet. SaaS incorporates both the IaaS and the PaaS model. In this model, all customers are given access to a single copy of an application which was created specially for SaaS distribution. All customers have same application source code and in events of new updates, all customers are given the access. Based on the service level agreement between the customer and the provider, a customer's data may be stored locally, in the cloud or both in the cloud and locally. An organization for example, can create its own software and integrate the software tools with SaaS using the SaaS provider APIs. We have

SaaS applications for vital business technologies like sales management, email, financial management, customer relationship management (CRM), billing and collaboration as well as Human resource management (HRM). Some tope SaaS providers are Oracle, Salesforce, Microsoft, Intuit and SAP.

In summary, SaaS lets users have easy access to software applications like emails etc over the internet.

Benefits of SaaS

- The software is available on demand globally and can be accessed over the Internet via browsers.
- Although in some cases a flat fee may be charged coupled with a

maintenance fee, a typical SaaS license is subscription-based or usage-based and is billed on recurrently.

- Both software and service are monitored and maintained by the provider with no regard to where the various software components are running. A code on the client's side which is executable may exist, but the maintenance of the code or its interaction with the service isn't the client's responsibility.
- Distribution, maintenance and minimal end-user system costs are generally reduced with the SaaS service applications thus making it a lot cheaper.

- SaaS applications include features like automated updates, upgrades, and patch management.
- It is known that SaaS applications sometimes have a far lower entry barrier, an ability to scale on-demand and at a recurring cost as opposed to their locally installed adversaries.
- Software version is the same for all users in order for them to be compatible with each other.
- Multiple users are supported by SaaS which provides a shared data model through a multi-tenancy model at a single-instance.

The Platform as a Service (PaaS)

Platform as a Service (PaaS) is a type of cloud computing where third party provides both software and hardware tools over the internet, this mostly applies to software for application development. The service provider hosts the software and hardware on infrastructure belonging to the host. This alone makes users free from installing software and hardware in-house to run or develop a new application.

With PaaS, a business entire IT infrastructure are not replaced rather the business gets its key services from PaaS. This include Java development or application hosting.

A PaaS provider creates and supplies a strong and improved environment for users to be able to install applications and data sets. Rather than worrying about building and managing infrastructures and services, businesses are able to focus on building and running applications.

Most products under PaaS are built towards software development. From this platform, we get storage infrastructure along with version management, text editing, compiling and text services that aids developers to create improved and better software.

A very good example of Platform as a Service (PaaS) according to the given explanation will be SQL database, Microsoft's Azure.

Systems for PaaS could be anything from developer platforms like Windows Azure Platform to systems like Drupal, Squarespace, Wolf, and others where the tools are modules that are very well developed with nearly no need for coding.

That being said, PaaS models include a good number of services, amongst which are:

- **Development of Applications:** PaaS creates a means for user-crafted programs to be in supported language or for a visual development environment to have the code written for you.

- **Collaborative capability:** many users can use PaaS systems as a means to collectively work on the same projects and/or share resources.
- **Management of data:** accessing and using of data in data store is made possible by using provided tools set for that purpose, and data can be stored in either the service of the PaaS provider's or a third-party storage service.
- **Instrumentation, performance, and testing:** for applications, tools are made available for the measuring and optimization of the user's performance.
- **Transaction management:** services such as transaction management or

brokerage are provided for by most PaaS systems. This provides for the maintenance of transaction integrity.

As the vibrancy of PaaS third party add-ons, applications, tools, services and associated markets ascend, the better they are, and these functionalities allow you to extend your application via purchase of functionality which is in most cases cheaper than rolling your own. The tools needed to construct different types of applications are provided by the PaaS for the enablement of working together in the same environment, among which the most common application types are:

- Composite business applications

- Data portals
- Mash-ups of multiple data sources

Data sharing must be enabled in these applications to allow it run in a multi-tenant environment and help the applications work in tandem much easier which is why, a common development language such as Java or Python is usually offered.

The Infrastructure as a Service (IaaS)

Infrastructure as a Service (IaaS), is the most comprehensive of all the cloud computing models. In the IaaS, the customers are given liberty to utilize and run as many software as they need such as operating applications and systems, given that they have the backing of the suppliers who provide all the required networks storage, processing, and other necessary resources for computing. The customers have absolute power over the operating systems such as implemented application and space. Here, a computer environment or infrastructure (preferably called software and hardware) is provided for by this Cloud computing model.

In summary, Infrastructure as a Service (IaaS) is a cloud computing service model in which the cloud virtualizes hardware. In this particular model, the servers, storage, network infrastructure, and so forth are owned by the service vendor.

The payment scheme here is also defined and incurred based on usage, meaning that users only pay for services used at the rate of storage per gigabytes just like internet mobile data is calculated in gigabytes and similarly data transfer or usage computing per hour. An example which best suits this type of Infrastructure as a Service (IaaS) based on the above statements is Firewall hosts. Another example of the IaaS is the Amazon's Web Services Elastic Compute Cloud (EC2) or Secure Storage Service (S3)

Benefits of the IaaS:

- **Saves Cost:** an obvious pro of using the IaaS model is the reduction in cost of infrastructure. Given that the IaaS is based on a metered system of charging customers, organizations choose to use this service model as they no longer have to worry about ensuring their system stays running, hardware maintenance, replacing of old equipment etc. The IaaS is also sort after as it requires no upfront payment, or charges for unused services.

- **Flexible scalability:** the IaaS is preferred in the eyes of its users due to its ability to scale up when more systems are needed and scaling down to release these virtual systems into the Cloud all in a bid to suit the user's current needs. This on-demand flexible scalability helps the IaaS respond with agility to the possibly constant change in a customer's requirements, a feature which is good for running expendable tests.

- **Fast Response Time:** thanks to the agility of the IaaS in responding to needs, user organizations can respond to client needs quicker than their competitors thus keeping them ahead of the curve in terms of productivity and delivery.

- **Support for Disaster Recovery, Back Up and high availability:** this simply means the IaaS has very versatile and prolific measures put together as a fail-safe plan in case of a disaster which would have in other cases of computing methods caused them to lose data and/or cost them so much money on recovery. This includes everything the organization needs to function as usual and at a recovery speed that turns what would have been a hole in productivity to merely a road bump.

- **Focus on business growth:** with all of the above stated weight and responsibilities taken off the shoulders of the users, they gain more time to focus on the business whilst saving time, money and energy which can now be invested in productivity without the unnecessary worry like- data loss, security, and cost of maintenance etc. that come with other forms of computing.

Amongst these three service models, it is easily noticeable that IaaS is the service model out of the rest that has maximum control over the infrastructure providers. When put in comparison with IaaS, PaaS has far lesser control over the infrastructure providers. Every service the IaaS offers its clients, are part and parcel of the responsibilities of the Cloud provider.

SaaS, which is provided to its customers through a network, gives its customers very little control over the infrastructure when they make use of this service. The control and management of the fundamental infrastructure and platform is a task set aside and is part of the Cloud providers' responsibilities.

Chap 3: Virtualization of Service models

What is virtualization?

Virtualization simply refers to the creation of a non-physical version of a server, operating system, storage devices or network resources, with the full capabilities of the physical one but without the hardware unit. Think of it like 'Faith', you can have it, base belief on it, use it, but in actuality it isn't a physical thing you can hold irrespective of the fact that it exists.

Virtualization is a technique that allows different users, organizations and customers to share a single physical instance of an application or a resource.

This is done simply by giving a logical name to the physical storage then create pointers that users, customers can use to access the physical storage when needed.

Virtualization is aimed at the management of workloads by turning traditional computing into a more scalable, efficient and economical system of computing. Think of Virtualization of technology as the reduction of hardware which helps to save cost and energy.

What is the Concept Behind Virtualization?

Hardware virtualization is creating a virtual (non-physical) machine over already existing hardware and operating system. With a virtual machine, the environment is logically separated from its underlying hardware.

The Host Machine is the machine on which the virtual machine is created on while **Guest Machine** refers to the virtual machine itself.

Architecture of Virtualized Technology

Virtual allocation of computing space and/or memory is usually set aside for server users. These servers require a host (platform) on which a hypervisor (i.e. the software through which the hardware is interacted with) runs. The virtualized model is made up of users of Cloud computing, service models, virtualized models and its host software and their accompanying hardware. The virtualization software makes the running of multiple instances of operating systems and multiple applications on the same server at the same time, and is based on three stated service models which are; SAAS (software as a service), PAAS (platform as a service) and IAAS (infrastructure as a service).

- SAAS makes applications available to the cloud users as it suits their needs.
- PAAS gives the cloud users a common ground (platform) on which their applications can be executed.

- IAAS provides the Cloud's resources, the security and hardware required for their maintenance.

Two things to remember in virtualization are

Host: for virtualization purposes, the hypervisor software runs on a virtualization platform called the "Host".

Hypervisor: the software with which the virtual machine is being used to work under the virtually simulated environment is called "Hypervisor".

Comparing Traditional Servers to Virtual Servers
Basic Traditional Servers

These are usually managed by a system administrator and consist of an operating system, the hardware, the storage and the application. When this type of server becomes filled, it has to be replaced immediately.

Advantages of the Traditional Servers

a. Easy deployment

b. Back-up is easy

c. Can run applications virtually.

Disadvantages

a. Cost effectiveness of hardware maintenance.

b. Difficulty in replication.

c. Unable to update physical infrastructure.

d. Difficulty in implementation of redundancy.

Virtual Servers

Virtual servers deal with the software aspect of computing whilst doing away with the need for hardware. Virtual servers consist of an operating system, storage and an application.

Advantages of Virtual Servers

a. IT pool maintenance.

b. High availability of hardware.

c. Use of a virtually based environment.

d. Lesser heat and energy consumption as lesser hardware is used.

Types of Virtualization

Virtualization in Cloud computing can be done in fours ways as explained below:

1. Hardware Virtualization: When the Virtual machine manager (VMM) otherwise known as virtual machine software is installed directed on the hardware system, we call this hardware virtualization.

The key work of the hypervisor is to monitor and control the memory, processor as well as other hardware resources.

Once the virtualization of hardware system is done, installation of different operating systems become possible as well as running different apps on the OS.

Uses of Hardware Virtualization

This is mostly for server platforms, because it is easier to control virtual machines than it is to control physical servers.

2. Server Virtualization: When the Virtual machine manager (VMM) otherwise known as virtual machine software is installed directly on the Server System, we call this server virtualization.

Uses of Server Virtualization

This is done due to the ability of dividing a single physical server into multiple servers based on demand and also for balancing weight load.

3. Operating System Virtualization: When the Virtual machine manager (VMM) otherwise known as virtual machine software is installed on the Host Operating system rather than the hardware system, we call this operating system virtualization.

Uses

This is used mostly to test applications on different OS platforms.

4. Storage Virtualization: has to do with the grouping of physical storage from several network storage devices to make it look like it is a single storage device. This is implemented with the aid of software applications.

Uses

This type is mostly used to back-up and also for recovery purposes.

Why Virtualization?

We should virtualize because of the following reasons:

a. **Isolation:** it aids isolate users from each other thus even though they share the same software, all of a user's personal data isn't exposed; thereby making open collaborations easier.

b. **Resource sharing:** Huge amounts of resources can be dissected into redundant virtual resources so that multiple users can use it via virtualization techniques.

c. **Dynamical resources:** unlike the difficulties experienced with the traditional servers when it comes to reallocation of resources, it is quite easy to reallocate resources ranging from storage, to computational resources.

d.   **Resource Aggregation:** the small available resources, through virtualization, can be increased to a larger extent.

Chap 4: Characteristics, Benefits, Advantages and Disadvantages of Cloud computing

A lot of aging concepts of technology come together to form the building blocks of Cloud computing which can make it difficult for the new generation of technology savvies and/or users who are new to the whole Cloud computing concept, find it easy to understand. Cloud computing is obviously revolutionary and comes with benefiting characteristics which could enable users know the technological know-how on how to utilize it with full optimization.

Among these characteristics include:

- The Paradigm Shift in Cloud computing:

On choosing a Cloud service provider, a good portion of what is an enormous infrastructure of linked computer storages, network capacities and actively functioning data centers, would be leased to you for as long as you use and pay for it. Most of these data centers are run by large multi-million-dollar companies. There's been estimate of how much a state-of-the-art microchip facility can cost which is anywhere between 2 to 5 billion dollars (this estimate was done to aid you get a whiff of the scaling). Most large providers of Cloud computing service have multiple data centers located everywhere in the globe, and by comparison, a Cloud computing data center can be run with the cost range of 100 million dollars (this is for state-of-the-art data centers). Usually, more accurate counts of data centers are often difficult to obtain, but it's known that Google has at least 35 data centers whilst Amazon's web services Cloud has at least 20 data centers; both of which are situated worldwide.

The American military created an initiative in the 1960s whose primary focus was the reduction of electronics. This initiative saw that funds were inputted into a good number of the semiconductor lines of production, thus leading to the creation of advanced microprocessors, dense memory arrays, and the sophisticated integrated circuit technology used in making computers, and mobile devices and a lot more of present-day technological devices. A good number of large companies were forced or rather coaxed by the commercialization of the internet, to build gigantic computing infrastructures to give their businesses the required support.

The infrastructure, that is, 'Amazon.com', was built to support elasticity in demand to allow the systems accommodate traffic peaks on busy shopping days such as "Black Friday". Amazon had to open its network to partners and customers as **Amazon web services** due to the capacity idleness it underwent.

On the other end, Google's business has overtime experienced an exponential growth that has prompted it to set up and build a worldwide array of data centers. Built in 2006, one of Google's data center situated in Dallas, Oregon, is said to be the size of an American football field.

Whilst these data centers have in their various ways increased in size, other businesses have grown their Cloud computing data centers as "Greenfield" projects. It is noticeable that these data centers have been known to take these into consideration when setting up site:

i) Have proximity to water in abundance.

ii) Ensure that system latency is completely optimized.

iii) Situate centers where there are high-speed network backbone connections.

iv) Ensure power cost in situated area is low

v) Gain leverage of renewable power supply.

vi) Be unobtrusive in terms of keeping costs of land and occupation modest

vii) Obtain tax breaks.

If all the above stated are provided, there's little to absolutely no chance that the efficiency of a Cloud computing networks in the data centers would be flawed given that this would enable the making of utility computing profitable as it captures enough margin.

These companies are quite big energy consumers as they consume roughly about 10 percent of the world's total power. These companies like Google for instance may become major players in the 21st century production of energy. Cloud computing has become such a big deal thanks to the internet's creation of technological utilities.

Services and applications that aid productivity which are delivered online as Cloud computing applications have undergone proliferation over the last couple of years. Regardless of the fact that not a lot of people implement the once straightforward client-to-server deployment of the internet, Cloud computing still has exemplary impact which abounds in our everyday life.

In many cases, the same applications which are Cloud hosted support the on-premises deployment and the transparent movements of said applications to the Cloud.

A case study is *Channeladvisor.com*. Their auction listings and sales management have been known to have many users. The site recently included a CRM connector to *salesforce.com* after its expansion to include more services.

Thanks to Cloud computing, software delivery has experienced a major shift in the economics in a manner quite similar to that of how music streaming caused the shift in the delivery of commercial music. Cloud computing has enabled new vendors of software the ability to create productivity aiding applications at prices much lower than would be possible before now due to the advantages in Cloud computing. Given the decline in the number of bib box computer stores alongside the purchase of older and orthodox retail computer models, gaining a market to sell said system types has become increasingly difficult for them. Take Wal-Mart vendors as a case study.

Meanwhile, the much more sort after new models of computer applications allows vendors, like Google, to offer applications like complete office suites for free to people, individually; with the support of the subscription models of their advertiser. Google itself as a business has had some major successes in comparison to the industry leader, Microsoft Office. Few years ago, this partly caused the Los Angeles County' switch to Google Docs.

According to the Definition of Cloud Computing by NIST, as earlier stated, the classification of cloud computing sub-sections into three SPI service models (SaaS, IaaS, and PaaS) and four cloud types (public, private, community, and hybrid) and also assigns five essential cloud computing characteristics that systems must render:

- **On-demand self-service:** provisions for computer resources can be made available with no need for interaction with personnel of the Cloud service provider. Computing capabilities, which include server time and/or network storage, can unilaterally be provided for by users without supervision of the Cloud's service provider or any other human middleman's interaction.

- **Broad network access:** even with the most standard of methods, resources available on the Cloud are easily accessible and enable clients of all ramifications the provision of platform-independent access.

More so, the access is available to clients irrespective of device which could range from heterogeneous operating systems to devices such as laptops and mobile phones. These computing capabilities are available via the internet or networks which are easily accessible via the utilization of standard and channelled mechanism, all of which is made to encourage people to make use of heterogeneous platforms.

- **Resource pooling:** resources which are created by the provider of the Cloud service are pooled together in a system which supports multi-tenant usage. All of the systems, both physical and virtual, are allocated or reallocated dynamically as required. This concept of pooling is the idea of abstraction that hides the location of resources such as virtual machines, processing, memory, storage, and network bandwidth and connectivity. The provider's computing resources serve multiple users after being pooled together. Location independence is not a luxury the customers enjoy here as they have no control neither are they knowledgeable about the exact location of the services they are being provided with, although they might be able to specify the location at a higher abstraction level.

- **Rapid elasticity:** Resources can be provisioned for at a rate that is both rapid and elastic. These resources can be added by the systems when they either, scale up the systems thus adding more powerful computers or scaling out the systems with computers of the same kind. The demands from customers gain commensuration from the scaling of systems given that the scaling may either be automatic or manual depending on the client's standpoint. Cloud computing is a limitless resource pooling system which can be acquired via purchase at any time and any desired quantity, as is their resources.

- **Measured service:** The use of cloud system resources is measured, audited, and reported to the customer based on a metered system. Using a standardized metric system such as storage usage amount, transaction number, bandwidth or network I/O (Input/Output), a client can incur charges based on a good range of rate types including processing power used. Charges are incurred by the client only for the services they use. In this situation, Cloud computing systems are automatically controlled with optimization for the leveraged resources. Given the already mentioned metering capabilities which are utilized for abstraction, a lot can be done by resources example monitoring, controlling and making provision for data transparency, for the user as well as its provider as far as service implementation is concerned.

Benefits of cloud computing
It's well-known that the features/characteristics of cloud computing listed

above can as well be seen as benefits of using cloud computing but we thought it'd be of added value to you to list the following additional advantages:

- **Ease of utilization:** quite often, depending on the type of service you're being offered by your Cloud computing service provider, you may get to realize that you do not require hardware or software licenses to implement the services received.

- **Simplification of maintenance and upgrade:** patches and upgrades are much more easily applied thanks to how centralized the systems are. This means access and updates are given freely to users who seek to keep their software up to date.

- **Quality of Service:** under contract, the quality of service is negotiable whilst purchasing Cloud computing services from a vendor. You can ask for the service to be optimized to meet your needs.

- **Reliability:** the ability of Cloud computing networks to upscale or downsize, and be open to optimization to meet users' needs with no more pressure or expenditure than required whilst balancing load makes them so much more reliable, even more reliable than one can be achieved by a single organization.

- **Lower Costs:** it is common knowledge around these parts that Cloud computing networks and services alike are created to run at higher efficiencies and greater utilization with inversely proportional costs while being effortlessly reliable.

- **Low Barrier to Entry:** with Cloud computing it doesn't cost much to setup a network and get things running. Regardless of how little one starts or how little the upfront start-up capital expenditure is, with Cloud computing, one can easily expand to a big size in little to no time without the unnecessary fears that come with hardware networking.

- **Outsourced IT management:** in cloud computing, you can easily use the deployment model feature which outsources to third party to manage your computing infrastructure while you focus on the actual running of the business aspect with far lesser fear of security issues. In most cases, you save cost from employing IT staffs.

Disadvantages of cloud computing
The advantages are numerous, however, like many other computing systems, Cloud computing has its fair share of disadvantages.

- Even with the number of benefits of Cloud computing being multitudinous, there are just as many disadvantages as there are advantages. Generally, there's a colloquial rule that the Cloud computing advantages have to present a mire coaxing and compelling pitch for small organizations than is required when pitching to larger ones. There's usually support for IT staff and efforts for development provided for by these larger companies that create room for software solutions which are created to cater peculiar issues and particular needs.

- When a service in the Cloud or an application is being put into use by you, you are utilizing something that isn't technically as customizable as you might want it to. In addition, applications which are deployed on-premise still carry many more features in comparison to their

Cloud counterparts although in many cases, these Cloud applications also have this capability.

- All Cloud computing applications have been known to suffer from inherent latency which is actually an intrinsic part of the connectivity of their Wide Area Networks. Though Cloud computing applications are known to do marvellously well when it comes to large-scale processing of tasks, Cloud computing isn't a good model suggestion if the applications you run require large amounts of data transfer.

- Also, just like the internet, Cloud computing is a stateless system because it is virtual thus information is necessarily unidirectional in nature in order for communication to be able to survive on distributed systems. The service provider receives all your requests in the forms of 'HTTP:', PUTs, GETs, and so on, to which you wait on the service provider who then sends a response using what may seem as a conversation between client and provider, but in actuality is done with a disconnect between the two. Now, this disconnect creates a gap, thus causing messages to travel over multiple routes and resulting in the data's arrival to be out of sequence. Regardless, when this happens, many other known characteristics of Cloud computing aid the communication to still succeed despite the medium's faultiness. Therefore, for transactional coherency to be imposed upon the system, transaction managers, service brokers, and other forms of middleware must be added to the system as additional overhead and this can easily lead to an introduction of a very large amount of performance hit on some applications.

- Privacy and security would undoubtedly be an area of common interest to most Cloud computing users. As your data travels over and rest on systems that are no longer within your power or authoritative control, there's a risk tendency of data getting into the wrong hands due to the occurrence of interception of others and this is why you would not be able to count on the vendor or Cloud provider to maintain your privacy especially when faced with governmental actions. Remember this is just a tendency.

Take the United States as a case study with focus on the millions of phone calls which ran from AT&T and Verizon that was extracted by the National Security Agency using a data analyser to extract security matching phone calls.

Another good example is the Chinese case with Google services, which had undergone a content removal filter that caused the government of China to step in and object.

All of this occurred because Google realized, after five years of operation that Chinese hackers were breaking into and accessing Gmail accounts of Chinese citizens and all of this ended as Google had to move their servers from Google.ch to Hong Kong.

So, whilst the Cloud computing industry continually undergoes redress to both old and new security threats and concerns, if you work with sensitive data it is advised that you be aware, particularly of the issues involved just so you can make a wiser computing services decision.

- Nowadays, more and more organizations get faced with a plethora of regulatory compliance issues. In the United States, companies must act in compliances with the Sarbanes-Oxley Act as a major part of their accounting requirements. Such requirement may take different forms for different example; health care providers have data privacy rules by the HIPAA to which they must be in compliance to. In Europe, the European Common Market has a boat-full of its own legislation that companies have to deal with too. Said rules apply to data in transit differently from as they do data at rest. Having said that, in situations where data is being run through lines that cut across multiple states and/or countries, you may suffer with having to comply with multiple jurisdiction issues. Not much support can be expected from Cloud computing system vendors in such cases where the government is involved, and this causes much of the burden sometimes the entire burden to be put on the client. In a big paraphrase, Cloud computing is a risky area to go to in terms of compliances.

Understanding Cloud Architecture

Naturally, Cloud computing is an extension of various principles of designs, protocols and systems which have developed over the course of the past 20 years. Cloud computing displays some new abilities which are designed into an application stack with responsibility for resource programmability, scalability and virtualization. The composability characteristics of Cloud computing is a term used to describe the Cloud's ability to build applications from component parts. A platform can be said to be a Cloud computing service in that it has both hardware and software, and can be used to create more complex software with virtual appliances.

A set of protocols (many of which are standard internet protocols) with which the various layers of software, hardware and client communications, is required by Cloud computing. In order to manage and inter-process communications that have grown overtime, Cloud computing relies on a set of protocols of which the most commonly used is the *XML* which is commonly used as a format for messaging, the *Simple Object Access Protocol (SOAP)* which is used as an object model and the *Web Services Description Language (WSDL)* which is a set of discovery and description protocol tool used to manage transactions.

Chap 4: Exploring the Cloud Computing Stack

Cloud computing can be broken down into two architectural layers:

- A client as a front end
- The "cloud" as a backend

The above stated descriptions are the two basic layers of what actually comprises of multiple component layers and complementary functionalities with a fine mixture of standard and proprietary protocols. In some cases, Cloud computing may be distinguished from older models using the *Application Programming Interface (API)* which often controls the information technology service and helps modify the delivered services on the network.

Under this, we would look at 6 ways of exploring the cloud computing stacks listed here:

- Composability
- Infrastructure
- Platforms
- Virtual Appliances
- Communication Protocols
- Applications

Composability

Cloud-built applications often have a collection of components that build a property. This feature is referred to as composability. Services which can be tailored for specific purposes using standard parts are assembled using components of a composable system. These composable component must be:

- **Modular:** it is an independently cooperative and self-contained unit which is reusable, and replaceable.

- **Stateless:** it can undergo and execute a transaction with no effect or regard to other transactions and/or requests.

Transactions are required to be stateless. A couple of Cloud computing applications can through brokers, service buses and transaction monitors, provide managed states and in more peculiar cases, full transactional systems are deployed in the Clouds although this would be hard to architect in distributed architecture.

Although software and hardware composability are not necessarily a requirement in Cloud computing from the user or developer's standpoint, it is a highly sort after feature given that it makes implementation of system designs easier whilst making solutions more portable and interoperable.

Cloud computing systems have the tendency of reducing in composability for users as the incorporation of more services to the Cloud computing stack increases. For IaaS (Infrastructure as a Service) vendors such as Amazon Web Services, GoGrid, or Rackspace, there's no wisdom in offering to customers who are most certainly deploying applications on standard operating systems such as Linux,

Windows, Solaris, etc., non-standard machines.

The logic surrounding the idea that composability diminishes as you go up the Cloud computing stack is from the users' perspective because if you are a service provider of PaaS or SaaS, the responsibility of creating the platform or service to be presented to the reseller, user or developer, rests on your shoulder and this makes working with a composable system a very powerful notion.

That being said, a PaaS or SaaS service provider gets the same benefits that a user does—from a composable system. These benefits among other include:

- No difficulty in system assembling
- System development at cheaper costs
- More reliable operation
- A greater number of qualified developers
- A design methodology which is logical

The module itself can be written in any programming language that best suits the developer although this isn't always specified. From standpoint, the system module is more of a black box, in which only the interface is well specified. Thanks to this independence, the internal activities of the components and modules can be interchanged for a different model at will as long as the specifications of the interface remain the same.

Infrastructure

Providers of large Infrastructure as a Service (IaaS) are dependent on virtual machine technology for the delivery of servers for the running of applications. Described in terms of a machine image, virtual servers have been known to be described in terms of realistic servers with which a given number of microprocessor (CPU) cycles, network bandwidth and memory access can be delivered to customers. Said virtual machines serve as containment assigned specifically for resources and run the software which in turn defines the Cloud computing system utility.

Virtual servers present a new perspective in the programming of applications. For example, when software is being created, it requires several tasks to be performed in parallel, the programmer might write an application to create additional threads of execution that need be managed by the application. When a Cloud service application is created by a developer, they can have the best suited services attached to the application allowing it to scale the execution of the program.

Platforms

Platform in Cloud computing simply refers to a software layer that is used in the creation of service of a higher level. As we discussed earlier, many different Platform as a Service (PaaS) providers render services designed to give developers different capabilities. Cited here are three major PaaS examples:

- SalesForce.com's *Force.com* Platform
- Windows Azure Platform
- Google Apps and the Google App Engine

The difference between a platform and a virtual appliance is that the installed software is a construct of components and services controlled through an API that the platform provider publishes.

It is quite reasonable for system vendors to transfer their development environments to the Cloud with Web applications successfully created with similar technologies, therefore, NetBeans Integrated Development Environment (IDE) can be found to be included in a platform which is based on a Sun xVM hypervisor virtual machine which also supports the Sun GlassFish Web Stack and programmable using Perl or Ruby. Developers who use windows might be provided with a platform by Microsoft for them to be able to run a Hyper-VVM, use the ASP.NET framework, Support applications such as SQL (which is an enterprise application), and be Visual Studio programmable. This will allow for usable applications to be created in the Cloud for multiple users.

Often times, platforms come with a plethora of application design-aiding tools and utilities. Inclusively, one may also find developer tools for team collaboration, tools for storage, program and attribute measuring instrumentation, tools for testing, versioning, and tools for database and web service integration, all of which are dependent on the providing vendor.

Similar to how virtual appliances open themselves to users via an API, so also does a Cloud-built application which implements a platform service use the service through its own API. This will then allow for interaction between users and the platform as the service consumption is being carried out via the API thus making the scaling and management of the services to be carried out appropriately by the platform. HTML, JavaScript, etc. are sometimes offered to users of some platforms as interface development tools. More and more developers are choosing to work with rich internet environments such as Adobe Flash, Air, Flex, or other alternatives given to how increasingly the web has become media-oriented. The platform API gets abstracted away from user interface thus making the UI have to manage said services.

Virtual Appliances

The term "Virtual appliances" may be a little misleading because it gives the mental picture of a device with a narrow purpose. Virtual appliances are software which are installed on virtual servers. A virtual appliance is a platform instance which occupies the middle of the Cloud computing stack. Web Server applications, Database server applications, and the likes can run on a virtual machine images thus referred to as virtual appliances.

A virtual appliance is a deployment object common in the Cloud and is an area with considerable amount of activity and innovation. The ability to utilize appliances as basis for complex service assembling is a major advantage of virtual appliances given that the appliance is now one of your standardized components, thus aiding your system management to be easier as the need for application configuration and maintenance is removed.

Communication Protocols

Implemented standard Internet protocols alongside the underlying transfer protocols (like *HTTP* and *HTTPS*) aid in the rise of Cloud computing through services available on the internet.

Computed and data resources in the Cloud are easily exposed using standards and protocols which come in form of either format data or communications, which are sent over these 2 protocols. For inter-process communication (IPC) processes to be carried out, networking lines have had various client/server protocols applied to them during distribution over the years. Various forms of RPC (Remote Procedure Call) implementations (including DCOM, Java RMI, and CORBA) make effort to resolve issues involving service engagement and transaction management over what is a stateless network. Web-centric RPC technology's XML-RPC is its first service in which platform-independent XML data is used in the encoding of programmed calls which are carried over the HTTP (which is the networking transport all users are linked).

Thanks to WSDL and SOAP, web services are allowed to describe additional properties and methods they could provide all of which is made possible through the created WSDL and SOAP extensions. Said extensions are known under the name of WS-*, or the "WS-star". Among which include:

- WS-Addressing
- WS-Discovery
- WS-Eventing
- WS-Federation
- WS-MakeConnection
- WS-Messaging
- WS-MetadataExchange
- WS-Notification
- WS-Policy

- WS-ResourceFramework
- WS-Security
- WS-Transfer
- WS-Trust

Now, metadata can be added to SOAP messages thanks to the above stated specifications which serves as a standard for data adding by modifying message headers while simultaneously ensuring the body structure is untouched. Furthermore, the WSDL XML message has the standard method for metadata exchange added onto it.

These WS-* services gain access to the remote server applications using the SOAP protocol which carries over XML messages, in ways which are increasingly becoming more complex as opposed to earlier methods in which gateways like CGI are provided by clients or servers to aid access media contents on the servers thus making the servers get burdened by accepting and processing very complex requests from the current data communications or conversing with their clients on sophisticated negotiations which need the minimization of processing information as responses are being exchanged.

Applications

Despite the fact that there are many details in which a Cloud computing stack encapsulates, it is not good enough in terms of expressing and giving account of all considerations required of any deployment. Omissions are noticeable in the behaviour of distributed Web applications and the Internet protocols designed to serve as a stateless service (by that we mean the internet's design to respect each request as an independent transactions).

Greater percentage of the work needed to be carried out is done by computer systems that are stateful, despite the fact that stateless servers are easier for architects to draw-up and stateless transactions more resilient to outages.

Transaction servers, message queuing servers and other middleware have been designed to bridge the issues of having really hard development efforts going into the making of Web properties useful in commerce and focused on the creation of mechanisms which change a set of stateless transactions to stateful ones. This problem, to an extent, has been known to be common in Cloud computing thus needing the implementation of a variety of constructs to solve identified issues. That being said, these are the two most important concepts to which this issue is fixed:

- The notion of orchestration—that process flow can be choreographed as a service.

- The use of what is referred to as a service bus that controls cloud components.

As time goes on, further improved methods for the establishment of transactional integrity would possibly be developed to better suit Cloud computing, but for now, these are the standard methods to which are now part of the Service Oriented Architecture.

Chap 5: Connecting to the Cloud, Cloud Storage and Migration

Cloud computing services can be accessed in a number of ways the two most common of which are:

- A Web browser

- A proprietary application

These two are most commonly used as they can run on a server, a PC, a mobile device, or a cell phone. These devices similarly utilize this type of applications, this refers to how they exchange data using an insecure and transient medium. That being said, three basic methods for securing said connections are:

- Use a secure protocol to transfer data such as SSL (HTTPS), FTPS, or

IPsec, or connect using a secure shell such as SSH to connect a client to the cloud.
- Create a virtual connection using a virtual private network (VPN), or with a remote data transfer protocol such as Microsoft RDP or Citrix ICA, where the data is protected by a tunnelling mechanism.
- Encrypt the data so that even if the data is intercepted or sniffed, the data will not be meaningful.

Clients who want the best connections rely on at least two of the above stated techniques during their communication with the Cloud. Web services are being relied upon by clients to make available secure connections but as time goes on, there is likelihood that clients themselves will ensure a secure connection without the mentioned dependence.

Take a café's network connection for instance, it is noticed that in some cases access to systems on their network aren't protected by firewall; worse still, the firewall isn't properly configured. This is the reason people prefer to carry routers with properly configured firewalls with them because these routers also come with in-built VPNs.

To that, here are three other recommended VPNs for secure connection purposes:

- Hotspot VPN (http://www.hotspotvpn.com/)
- Anchor Free Hotspot Shield (http://hotspotshield.com/)
- Gbridge (http://www.gbridge.com/)

Cloud Storage

Cloud storage as the name implies refers to the service to which where data is managed, stored, and backed up remotely. Users can access the Cloud storage using a network (usually the internet is the go-to network) and also store files online which can be retrieved from any location and time via the internet. The files are being kept on an external server and made available by the provider company. This gives provider companies ease in terms of data storage although it can be quite costly. Users need to back-up their stored data because recovering Cloud-stored data is a lot slower than recovering data from a traditional back up. Cloud storage is the lower layer of Cloud computing system which supports the service of the other layers above it.

Popular Cloud Storage Options

Listed below are a couple of Cloud-based storage services many of which provide up-to gigabytes in storage space for free, with promise for additional space at a monthly fee. These Cloud storage services, like all Cloud storage services, provide a simple drag-and-drop system of access whilst ensuring that data is synced between all of the user's devices. They also let users with signed-up accounts collaborate with each other.

DROPBOX

Collaboration: Users of Dropbox are able to upload and share entire folders with fellow Dropbox users via the Dropbox web interface, the Dropbox desktop client or other supported apps and devices. These folders can be viewed by all collaborators of the given folder. A user can either choose to store a file privately for personal purposes or publicly to enable others gain access. Files set as

"Public" can be accessed by both Dropbox and non-Dropbox users. However, unlike Dropbox users, non-Drobox users must download the file to open or use it and any changes made to their copy of the folder will not reflect on that of the original Dropbox user's folder.

Mobile App Support: Devices such as phone and tablets can easily access documents using the Dropbox mobile app.

Storage: Dropbox offers 2GB of free storage.

Strengths

Its biggest strength would be its ease of use. One can simply share a document or folder by using their device's native share function. Also, Data recovery is far easier with Dropbox than with most options. You can also decide what data syncing speed you'd prefer.

Weaknesses

It offers one of the lowest amounts of free storage.

Google Drive

Collaboration: in order to access documents stored with this option, users must own an account. Every change in document by the creator or collaborator is automatically synced and reflected upon the document. You will be notified of every change in the document if you own it.

Mobile App Support: Google Drive is available on Androids with options of downloading application or accessing via web browsers. You can even share Google Drive files to your contacts.

Storage: Google Drive offers 5GB of free storage.

Strengths

Google Drive comes with a built-in editor for documents which help ease editing of documents without need for third-party apps. It can be accessed via other Cloud based apps like ES File Explorer which aids in sharing flexibility.

Weaknesses

Sharing is quite difficult here in comparison to Dropbox— you need to have the web application to set it up. Speed of uploads and syncing are greatly influenced by your network.

Microsoft SkyDrive

Collaboration: data can be shared and accessed via Microsoft SkyDrive with or without accounts. You can also live-edit data online.

Mobile App Support: SkyDrive can be accessed using both a Window's phone app and an iOS (iPhone/iPad) app. Users are enabled to view and share as well as edit and update files via phone or tablet. Third party iOS apps, such as Pages and Keynote can access SkyDrive files.

Storage: SkyDrive offers 7GB of free space.

Strengths

It is the biggest in comparison to the others listed here in terms of space and just like Google Drive, you can edit documents within the browser, without having to use a third-party application like Microsoft Word.

Weaknesses

The interface of SkyDrive is somewhat less user friendly than Dropbox and Google Drive.

Advantages of Cloud Storage

- Usability - Every Cloud storage service listed here is easy to use and is accessible on easy-to-get devices like PCs, Tablets Androids etc.
- Bandwidth - As opposed to the traditional methods of sharing documents singly via email, you can upload it once to the Cloud storage and then share the links to all proposed recipients.
- Accessibility - Stored files can be accessed from anywhere as long as you have an Internet connection.
- Capacity- Support for infinite expansion above the PB level.
- Disaster Recovery – Cloud–stored data can serve as backups in situations where data is lost by

accident. These data backups can be accessed remotely with the use of an internet connection.

- Cost Savings – as has been stated many times already, using Cloud storage will help you save a lot of time and money which would have been spent on things like hardware maintenance.

Disadvantages of Cloud Storage

- Usability – In as much as it is easy to use, it is also easy for simple mistakes to occur such as permanently yet unknowingly moving a file to the Cloud and deleting the Cloud copy without backup.

- Bandwidth – Several cloud storage services have a specific bandwidth allowance which may not suit a user's needs and after which if you surpass will incur extra charges.
- Accessibility – Data cannot be accessed in the absence of an internet connection.
- Data Security – The easier it is for data to be shared with many people the riskier it is for uses as sensitive data may be shared or leaked by mistake. Plus, the thought of the possibility of having private organization data escaping their

grasp is a real bother to organizations and other users.

Migrating to the Cloud

Given everything we've said about this revolutionary change in computing systems, it's only fair that we help you know how to successfully migrate to the Cloud, and also help you understand things to consider when moving. Here, I'll highlight the available options and strategic suggestions to aid your thought-process, among which you can choose to use during your migration process. There are fundamental components that are essential to all cloud migration initiatives

Migration Strategy Fundamentals:

- Ensure that your strategy covers all grounds both in research and in knowing what you want and why migrating to the Cloud would be good for your business.
- Fully study your applications and data types to know what system of Cloud storage best suits you and to expose inefficiencies in Cloud services for better optimization.
- If need be, ensure your business is structured or restructured to suit the best possible Cloud service it deserves.
- Understand completely, factors of Cloud computing like how responsibilities are being divided and how it relates to security policy

and risk mitigation, and develop policies and controls accordingly.

Cloud Migration Guide

After carefully ensuring your desire and strategy to switch matches with the above stated fundamentals, you'll see for yourself that picking a Cloud computing service with applications that provide you with the necessities you need, to migrate to will be a lot easier. Nevertheless, always bear in mind that your plan will most likely run into the need of an amendment.

The process of migration to the Cloud is thankfully flexible enough to enable caution. It is possible for you to not move all your data at once to the Cloud as most people do in some cases especially with the "hybrid model" which makes it possible for companies to move their applications to the cloud at their own pace. Migration may be complex depending on the model being migrated to and for beginners we recommend you use the smallest on the scale of complexity as possible.

5 most common application migration strategies are:

Re-hosting: this is basically the re-deployment of applications to a Cloud computing hardware environment, most likely after changes were made to the initially deployed app. This migration type tends to make provision for a Cloud migration solution that is fast and easy. One issue with this strategy is that the elasticity and scalability benefits that come with the IaaS are unavailable with a re-hosting deployment. Although customers prefer to do the re-hosting deployment process by themselves, there are automated tools which are set to serve as the solution to the above stated. Regardless of what they choose to do, once their applications get running on the Cloud, they have the tendency to become easier to re-architect and optimization.

Re-platforming: here, the user runs applications on the infrastructure of the Cloud provider. It allows users to make Cloud-related optimizations without incurring expenditure on the developer's cycles whilst changing the applications core architecture. Re-platforming is known to be Backwards compatible which means developers can reuse resources they liked in the past, resources like legacy programming languages, frameworks for development, caches of old codes. The downside here is that the PaaS market doesn't always make provision for familiar resources to be offered to developers.

Repurchasing: although this sometimes leads to doing away with legacy applications or platforms, thus making service delivered software to be commercially available. A development team needs to be kept at hand for situations that affects the way a business function. This option is used during migrations to SaaS platforms, the disadvantage is its inconsistency in naming, issues of interoperability and vendor lock-ins.

Refactoring / Re-architecting: here, the architecture and development of applications are re-created and re-imagined most likely using the preset features of PaaS. This usually leads to loss of legacy codes and familiar frameworks especially in cases where the primary aim was to add new features, scale, or performance that would be difficult to achieve in the existing environment. On the brighter side, it also means provision of state-of-the-art tools available on the provider's platform. Here, a switch in vendors can mean forfeiting nearly all if not all of a customer's re-architected applications.

Retiring: this simply refers to the discarding of IT portfolio which is no longer useful and can be turned off. This helps to save time and money as your team's attention would be more focused on aspects of the business that is being needed with no distraction or incurred cost for the things that users can do without.

Chapter 6: Cloud Computing Security, Business Continuity and Data Recovery

Cloud security covers a wide range of policies, control measures, technologies, applications implemented for the protection of data, virtualized IPs, services, applications and the associated infrastructure of the Cloud. It is often seen as an underlying domain of security concerning networks, computers and information; the last being the broadest of the areas.

Cloud security associated issues

Users of Cloud computing and Cloud storage are provided with the opportunity to have third-party data centers store and process their data whilst organizations use the many variations of service models (SaaS, PaaS, and IaaS) and deployment models (private, public, hybrid, and community). Therefore, issues concerning the Cloud and its security measures fall into 2 basic categories, which are:

- Security issues burdened on vendors of Cloud (organizations providing software, platform, or infrastructure-as-a-service via the cloud)
- Security issues burdened on customers of Cloud (companies or organizations who host applications or store data on the cloud).

However, the burden of the above stated is divided between the vendor who must ensure that they secure their infrastructures whilst protecting their client's data and applications, and the user who most ensure that their applications are fortified with good measures of authentication.

Research has shown that insider attacks are one of Cloud computing's biggest threat. Organizations lose their ability to have physical access to servers which host their applications or store their data when using public clouds. This puts sensitive data at risk from insider attacks. Cloud service vendors need to ensure that their employees and anyone else who will have access to Cloud data must be checked thoroughly. They must also monitor their data centers frequently for suspicious activity.

There's also a chance one user's private data can be viewed by others especially in situations where Cloud providers store more than one customer's data on the same server. In this case, Cloud service providers need to ensure that proper data isolation and logical storage segregation measures are being put in place.

The utilization of virtualization in Cloud infrastructure implementation is a cause for security concerns for customers of the Cloud service. These concerns include the potential compromise of the virtualization software (Hypervisor).

Cloud Security Controls

The architecture which builds-up Cloud security can be effective if only the right defensive measures are correctly placed. Security issues in the Cloud are usually addressed, managed and averted using security controls which are put in place to defend any system weakness consequently reducing attacks on the system. These controls include:

Deterrent controls

This set of controls serves as a warning sign. They are used to ward-off and warn potential threats and attackers of the impending consequences should they choose to continue.

Preventive controls

These set of controls strengthens the systems against threats by reducing and possibly eliminating vulnerabilities. The use of strong authentication on implementation of these set of controls greatly reduces unauthorized access.

Detective controls

These set of controls is used in the detection of threats. The detective controls inform the preventive or corrective controls about the issue so they can address it squarely. Intrusive detection and prevention measures are used by system and network security 'watchdogs' to detect and eliminate threats.

Corrective controls

Corrective controls basically curb threats thus reducing the damage the threats have caused. They come in during or after damage has occurred. They restore system backups and help rebuild compromised systems.

Dimensions of cloud security

Security controls need to be selected and used in proportions which match the threat at hand. This means one must assess the threats, system vulnerabilities and threat impacts before implementing security controls. Cloud Access Security

Brokers or CASBs, are software placed between users of cloud and applications of Cloud to help give account of application usage, data protection and to monitor all activities of Cloud. Listed below are the dimensions of Cloud security:

Identity management

Enterprises have identity management systems which helps them control access to information and resources. Providers of Cloud computing either integrate identity management system in their infrastructure or they use a biometric system of identification. Sometimes, they even implement identity management systems of their own. A good example is

CloudID which provides a Cloud-based privacy-preserving system of biometric identification. This is performed in encrypted domains to avoid hacking.

Physical security

All hardware components of Cloud computing are physically protected against unauthorized access, theft, interference, and all forms of natural disasters whilst ensuring sufficiency in supplies like electricity to avoid disruption. This is usually made possible by ensuring that their data centers are in a state-of-the-art condition always.

Personnel security

Information regarding personnel who work at data centers is usually handled by security personnel who check their information before, during, and after employment. The security personnel screens them before employment, watches their activities during and after the course of their employment.

Privacy

Cloud computing providers ensure that data such as credit card numbers are secured and/or encrypted with access given only to authorized users. Digital identities and all other credentials of a user must be protected alongside any data collected or produced by the customer as he uses the Cloud. Authorization to gain access must be controlled only by the owner in untrusted cloud environments. Only authorized users can access the sensitive data while others, including CSPs, should not gain any information of the data.

Cloud Vulnerability and Penetration Testing

In order to ensure that your service is hardened enough to protect data from threats it is recommended that you scan your service from both inside and outside and test it for penetration. Like physical servers, virtual servers should be hardened to prevent leakage of data, malware and other forms of exploit. In order to avoid violation of acceptable use policy, Cloud service vendors must authorize the scanning as they risk losing the service to termination when rules are not properly followed.

Integrity

Integrity of data simply refers to the accuracy and completeness of data. It demands that providers should ensure that their customer's data is not being tampered with illegally, modified improperly, deleted deliberately, or fabricated. It is within the rights of the customer to request a restore and/or repair of missing and/or corrupted data.

Encryption

In a practice called crypto-shredding, advanced encryption algorithms which have been applied into cloud computing to increase the protection of privacy can also be deleted when there is no more use of the data.

Types of Encryption

Attribute-Based Encryption (ABE):

This is a type of public-key encryption where the user's secret key and cyphertext depend on attributes to which a decryption cannot be done if the user key doesn't match the attributes.

Ciphertext-Policy ABE (CP-ABE):

The CP-ABE is an encryption type that is focused on the design of the access structure. Here, the 'encrypter' controls the access to the service.

Key-Policy ABE (KP-ABE)   :

KP-ABE attribute sets are used to translate encrypted texts and the private keys associated to the specified policy that users will have.

Fully homomorphic encryption (FHE):

Computations on encrypted data and the computation of the sum and product for encrypted data are made possible with fully homomorphic encryption without the need for decryption.

Searchable encryption (SE):

Searchable encryption is a cryptographic system that provides secure search functions over encrypted data. It can be classified into 2 categories: SE based on secret-key (or symmetric-key) cryptography, and SE based on public-key cryptography. Its symmetric-key builds indexes of keywords to answer user queries and this helps increase its efficiency.

Compliance and Cloud Computing

There are many laws and regulations concerning data usage and storage. Many of which are particular about controls such as strong access controls and audit trails. Cloud users must ensure that their providers comply completely with these laws to avoid loss of data in an event where their service is terminated due to lack of compliance. In places like the US, these laws include

- Payment Card Industry Data Security Standard (PCI DSS)
- Health Insurance Portability and Accountability Act (HIPAA)
- Sarbanes-Oxley Act, the Federal Information Security Management Act of 2002 (FISMA)
- Children's Online Privacy Protection Act of 1998, among others.

Business Continuity and Data Recovery

Business continuity and data recovery measures put in place in case of data loss are made available by the Cloud providers. The customers may be involved in the making or they may be allowed to view the plans. Joint continuity exercises are sometimes carried out to help simulate compromising scenarios and how well their recovery measures work.

Log and Audit Trail

Cloud providers usually work with their users to ensure that the logs and audit trails that they (the providers) produce are properly secured and maintained for as long as the customers choose. These logs and audits also need to be made available for forensic investigations.

In Legal and contractual issues

Cloud users have to ensure they negotiate properly with their providers about terms concerning incidents of data loss or compromise and how they will be resolved. These negotiations should also cover terms concerning intellectual properties, and end-of-service which refers to what and how data and applications are returned to the user.

Public records

Agencies are required by law to retain and make electronic records available especially in situations where they run into legal issues. Sometimes, law requires agencies to conform to the rules and practices set by a records-keeping agency.

Chap 7: Conclusion

From all that has been said in this book, cloud computing can be said to be the future of storage in the tech world.

Although it has its disadvantages, however the advantages far supersede these disadvantages.

I hope this book answers all the question you may have on cloud computing as well as help you make an informed decision on the best model of cloud computing fit for your business.

Thank you.

Other Books by Same Author
DeepFake Technology: Complete Guide to Deepfakes, Politics and Social Media

https://amzn.to/2LddlFk

Printed in Great Britain
by Amazon